MENTAL PAUSE

A Quick and Easy Guide to Better Decision Making

BRANDON WOFFINDEN

DEDICATION

With all of my heart, I would like to express my love and gratitude to my wife and children. I am truly blessed, and I look forward to every day they are part of my life. I would like to express my gratitude for my parents and teachers for the lessons that shaped me into the person I am today. Thank you for being the miraculous people that you are. A special thanks to Margaret Hartford and Kendall Woffinden for their efforts in making this book a reality. You are amazing! Thank you for your contribution!

CONTENTS

INTRODUCTION

Life is difficult, but it is even more difficult when we don't make good decisions. I wrote this book to share what I have learned throughout my life about making the "wrong" decision. I would like to welcome you all to my first book writing experience! My hope is to be able to portray my thoughts and ideas about making better decisions in a way that makes sense and can be easily applied to everyday life.

Ever since I was a child, I thought I had something to share with the world. It was probably a combination of my father telling me "Son, you're unique and special, just like everybody else," and kids at school saying things like "Way to go GENIUS" or "Nice one

SMART A$$." However, I never understood why they referenced my back side when they were complimenting me.   Either way, I took the compliments as they came!

PART I

The Decision Making Process

MENTAL PAUSE

A CLOSER LOOK

Besides my own human experience of making mistakes, I have spent the last 15 years working for the Utah Department of Corrections. I worked a variety of jobs within the department, from correctional officer at the prison, then became a pre-sentence investigation report writer, to parole and probation agent, and currently a mental health therapist. It has been amazing to me to see individuals come into the judicial system, serve their time, get released, then a short time later start the whole process over again. I wondered, what is it about people that causes this "revolving door" behavior?

I first thought was that this only happens to people inside the prison system, but as I began my work as a therapist, I realized this is common. I believe it has to do with our emotional response, our "fight, flight, or freeze" response.

Decisions are like throwing rocks in a pond. They always cause a ripple effect. The size of the rock we throw determines the size of the ripple we create. The rock represents our decision and the ripple represents the consequence of the decision. Rocks vary in size and weight and we get to decide what type of rock we are going to throw, just like we can determine the outcome of the decision we make.

For example, if we make a positive decision, we will experience positive consequences such as happiness, success, love, and freedom, to name a few. If we make a negative decision, or a decision which hinders our personal progress creating doubt, guilt, fear, and other feelings of inadequacy, we will experience negative consequences such as loneliness, isolation, addiction, and frustration. A lot of the decisions we make can even be semi neutral, such as what am I going to wear today, what should I make for dinner, or what TV show should I fall asleep to tonight.

I believe every decision we make affects something else. If I choose to eat breakfast then the ripple effects are that I'm putting nutrition into my body, getting energy, taking care of my hunger etc. If I decide to not eat breakfast then my ripple effects are the opposite. I am hungry and I have lower energy. My mood is one end result affected positively or negatively based on my decision. Generally, I am happier when I've had something to eat. The decision to eat breakfast may seem trivial in regard to all of the other things we need to attend to in life, but I it provides a good example for the entire process of decision-making; including the ripple effect that follows.

There may be times in our lives where we feel all we are doing is living consequences and we have no control. It is important to know that all ripple effects eventually smooth themselves out. While we are "riding out the waves (consequences)," try not to make new ones or at least new negative ones.

I know we have all heard the old saying of "stop and think" or "sit down and take some deep breaths" whenever we get upset or angry. This is great advice and helps us out a lot if we are able to apply it in the moment. But most of the time, we don't remember those things until afterwards, when it's too late. When we are in the midst of a situation, we make instinctive or emotional decisions. There usually isn't any "logic" without hindsight.

When I was thinking of a title for this book, I wanted to come up with something that would stick in people's mind. A title or "slogan" if you will, that might help interrupt the instinctual/emotional process long enough to realize what is going on. If I could get people to interrupt themselves in a stressful situation with the statement **"I need to go through a mental pause,"** *then there is a chance that the emotional response would break long enough to allow logic to enter in and hopefully change the behavior.* A mental pause is simply disengaging from a situation long enough to take some deep breaths or calming down before making any decisions.

Let's look at the process of how a decision is made. The foundation, consists of moral values or beliefs developed as a result of our education, familial situation, financial status, race, spiritual beliefs, culture, etc and specific life experiences. These beliefs set an individualized precedence for our behavior; a moral code that we continually build on for the rest of our lives.

Ideally, the decisions we make would reflect these moral values and often they do, but primarily emotions control our decisions. For example: I may value honesty, but there may have been a time as a child where I spilled milk and when asked "who spilled the milk?" I may have responded with "I don't know," or "I didn't do it," for fear that I would get in trouble. This generally is a self-preservation or "safety" response. It is automatic and originates in the deep limbic system of the brain- our emotional center, where our fight, flight, or freeze response is initiated. Just because I didn't tell the truth in the situation doesn't necessarily mean that I don't value honesty.

Anytime we react to a situation or respond from our "fight, flight, or freeze" response, we may regret it. The situation afterward frequently consists of either regretting the decision made, and/or thinking about a million things we could have done to improve the situation.

Here are some major values, themes or ideas that people may find important in their lives:

- Family
- Honesty
- Respect
- Freedom
- Belief in a Higher Power
- Education
- Work Ethic
- Money

ICEBERG

We organize these by importance based on what we have been taught, our life experiences, and our perception of those experiences. Our values and beliefs are at the core of our decision-making, guiding everything we do. For example, you would expect to see a person who values family; spending as much time with their family as possible. A person who values money would be spending time at work, setting up savings accounts, budgets and so on.

To illustrate the process we go through to make decisions, let's compare it to an iceberg. A very different iceberg than Dr. Sigmund Freud utilized. This iceberg represents the individual making the decision. The diagram shows that a person's action is a direct reflection of their core value.

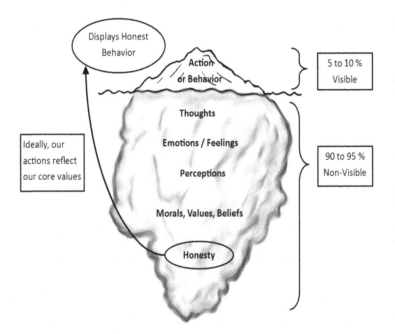

In addition to our core values and beliefs, we have perceptions, feelings, and thoughts that lead to actions. However, our actions are the only thing for which we ever experience tangible consequences. I could be upset with someone and be thinking of all kinds of things I'd like to do to them, but as long as I never acted on my feelings, I would not experience consequences.

As seen in the iceberg, actions only account for about 5-10% of the decision-making process. That leaves 90-95% under the surface or inside of us. So if we had control over our thoughts and feelings, we could control how we acted or reacted and essentially never have any regrets about our decisions. To help put this in perspective, imagine that you are going to Las Vegas and you had a 90-95% percent chance you would win the million dollar jackpot. Most people would take that bet.

Look how important it is for us to have control over our thoughts and feelings. When we have control of thoughts and feelings, it gives us the opportunity to take a mental pause and workout the issue inside ourselves before we react on our emotions. Once we act, we can't take it back and then we experience the consequences which come as a result of that action.

Why do we not always act from our core beliefs and values? One main reason may be that we don't feel safe. I work with both perpetrators and survivors of domestic violence and they have taught me *that people either tell the truth or don't tell the truth depending on how safe they feel. The fear of consequences plays a major role in how a person acts.*

Let's use a soccer game to demonstrate the decision-making process. If *I* was able to kick the ball and make a straight shot from center field to the other side of the field right into the goal, that would be much like having the value of honesty and never lying.

You would be completely honest when your partner asks you how you like the new recipe they made. Remember what I said about safety? We are only as honest as we are safe.

So in soccer we kick the ball and the other team blocked it, players kick it from side to side, up and down the field. This process can go on for ten to fifteen minutes, possibly longer, before the ball is slammed into the goal after a great pass, or gets kicked "out of bounds."

In the center or the core of each person are individual beliefs, morals, and values, which affect all aspects of decision making. Imagine that inside each of us is an "internal soccer game." The ball (drive, desire, or intention) gets kicked from center field (our morals and values). The end result is the goal, the ball going out of bounds, or even an injury (our action). Once the soccer ball (our intention) is released, the pathway to action is blocked by the opposing team (perceptions/attitudes, feelings/emotions, and thoughts).

Perceptions represent the first opposition in our soccer game. Perceptions are formed by our experiences. For example, when I was a law enforcement agent for adult probation and parole, I went to do a routine home visit to a lady on probation. My partner and I were invited into the home where my client and her 5-year-old daughter were living. Although it was a routine visit, my partner and I were outfitted in our bulletproof vests with our firearms strapped on our side, which could be intimidating and overwhelming for a child. As we walked down the stairs and rounded the corner the daughter froze with a look of shock and horror on her face. She began crying when she saw us.

What kind of messages has this child been getting in regard to police officers? Whenever there is a law enforcement officer around, mom goes to jail. If the child continues to have similar experiences throughout their lifetime, their perception of law enforcement will be negative.

In a shopping center, law enforcement officers help reunite a lost child with their parent. As this child grows up and has similar experiences, their perception of law enforcement will be positive.

Each child's experiences formed their perceptions from which they see the world. There is nothing wrong or right about either of them, it just is how it is. Sometimes our perceptions can block us from living successful happy lives. Sometimes we are taught things that aren't true. Sometimes we are taught things that go against our morals and values.

If I grew up in a home that every time we went to the grocery store I watched my mother stealing, then I learn and believe that stealing is what we do when we go to the store. All of the negative consequences that come from that action start to control my life. I start a life cycle of stealing, getting busted, and going to jail. Eventually I'm living a life comprised of negative consequences for decisions made.

It is the responsibility of every person to evaluate what they were taught growing up to see if their belief system matches their own personal values or if they are beliefs they have adopted for themselves from someone else. To do this, we need to ask questions like: Does that perception work for me?, Is that the career path I want to follow? Do my beliefs continually cause me problems or conflicts with others or do they help me live a happy life? One of my favorite books on this topic is "**The Voice Of Knowledge**" by Don Miguel Ruiz.

The next obstacle our internal soccer game runs into is emotions. Emotions play a major role in our behavior because it is our emotions that drive our thoughts. Have you ever been in a situation where your emotions drove your actions? Ever been out with a group of friends at a bar having a great time, then doing something you regretted?
 Or have you ever overreacted when arguing with your partner? What happened after you calmed down and came to your senses? Usually feelings of regret, guilt, and shame, as you leave imagining all the other ways you could have handled the

situation, and how much better it would have turned out. This kind of scenario indicates that our decisions are determined by emotion. The diagram below shows our actions do not always reflect core values.

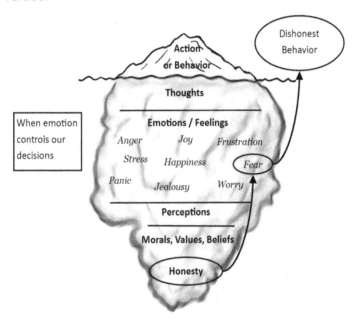

DECISION MAKING TEETER-TOTTER

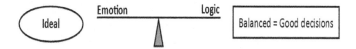

Another analogy to help illustrate decision-making is a scale or a "teeter-totter." On one side you have logic. On the other side you have emotion. There are a lot of times where our logic and our emotion are balanced. When our emotions and logic are balanced, we generally make good decisions. We can feel feelings, we can think thoughts, and our conclusions are pretty well-rounded. But what happens to our logic when our emotions rise and get stronger? Our logic hits the ground; it's out of the picture. It's like someone just flipped the light switch and the logic turned off.

This process happens to all of us. There isn't anyone that doesn't wrestle with overwhelming emotions; that is part of our life experience. Now our emotion is heightened and our logic decreases.

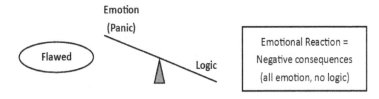

Making decisions while emotional is exactly what we are trying to stop doing because of all the negative consequences attached to them. The trick (where **"Going Through a Mental Pause"** comes in) is to not make any decisions while we are overly emotional. When our "fight-flight or freeze" response engages, we need some sort of action to disrupt this process. For example, when I am driving and a person cuts me off on the freeway, I feel a rush of anger and my first impulse is to speed up and hit them with my car. When I take a **"mental pause"** and think of the consequences I would suffer if I did hit someone deliberately with my car, I decide that making that particular decision is not worth it.

Thoughts are the next item on our list of obstacles. If our thoughts are driven by emotions, and if entertained long enough, they will lead to irrational or aggressive behaviors. At that point, there is no "taking it back." Consequences result from these actions and it feels like our life is nothing but living with the ripple effects of that negative decision.

Going through a "Mental Pause" is recognizing when you are getting emotional, getting some distance, calming down and allowing your logic ("Mental Abilities") to re-engage. If I have the thought, "I could get away with it," I automatically know that thought is driven by emotion because if I was doing what I'm supposed to there would be "nothing to get away with."

Let's say that a man just lost his job and his kids are hungry. He is in the grocery store and is stressed about not having a job and worrying about all the bills he has to pay. He's feeling anxiety and worry because he doesn't know what he's going to feed his family. Panic because he doesn't know how he's going to pay the rent. So his value of family responsibilities jumps to the top. Here is the list of values previously used. I'm using this now to illustrate how we can sacrifice things we value.

- Family
- Honesty
- Respect
- Freedom
- Belief in a Higher Power
- Education
- Work Ethic
- Money

The kicker is that if he allows the emotions of panic and stress to guide his decision, he may take action in the store (steal something) that will have a trail of negative consequences. In addition, he might go to jail, pay fines, pay attorneys, etc., which would deeply and thoroughly affect his family. When our emotions dictate our values, they will always sabotage our life.

Let's look at the scenario again. Say he "stole" for family. The wrong thing for the right reason quandary. What values is he sacrificing as a result of that action? His value of honesty, respect, money, freedom. He is also sacrificing his value of family because of the hardship they will endure.

Isn't that ironic? Even though he stole for his family (the right reason), *the decision was driven by emotion*, and therefore the whole thing backfired, jeopardizing all values, including family.

It is important for each one of us to love ourselves and hold on to the values and beliefs we find important.   A lot of people confuse self loving with being selfish. Selfishness is taking care of our own needs at the expense of someone else. Self loving sets a healthy boundary so that we are not taken advantage of; we need to give ourselves an appropriate amount of self care so we can meet our obligations and be a responsible citizen.

We don't want to sacrifice personal values, we want to have them all. That is not a selfish thing, it isn't at the expense of anyone else. It is a self loving thing. We all deserve to have the things we want and not sacrifice the things that are important to us because of our emotional decisions.. That is why it is so critical to go through a **"Mental Pause."**

If the man in the store was able to apply the use of a **"Mental Pause,"** he may have been able to come up with some better solutions for his issue; like utilizing State or Federal resources that could help with housing and unemployment benefits or accessing the local food bank or community church for financial help and food. The decision teeter-totter might look more like this:

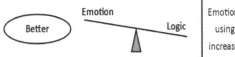

Emotional with some logic = using "Mental Pause" to increase logic before we act

Even after a mental pause, we can still be very emotional, but as long as we can access our logic we usually do ok. If I have a disagreement with someone, I will still be upset, but if I've allowed myself to take a **"Mental Pause"** so that logic influences my decision, then I "throw my positive rock in the pond instead of a negative one."

Emotions weigh heavily on our bodies. Remember how it felt when we rode the roller coaster for the first time? Or when we were really excited about going out on a date? We all have physical manifestations of our emotions. Some of these physical manifestations include increased heart rate, queasy stomach, sweating, and experiencing "tunnel vision." We experience these physical sensations whether we are excited and joyful or angry. The body merely alerts us that we are emotional. The sensations are the same either way.

Being able to recognize when we are emotional is the first part of utilizing the **"Mental Pause."** Once we recognize that the intense feelings we are having are our natural response to a stressful situation, we can do our best to get away from the situation, breath, calm down, and then start assessing why we feel that way. Once we have taken that **"Mental Pause,"** we can go back to the situation with our logic intact and balancing our emotions, we now solve the issue at hand.

PART II

Ways to Improve Thinking

MENTAL PAUSE

REQUIREMENTS AND EXPECTATIONS

What are the times we are most disappointed, upset, or angry? Usually when our expectations aren't being met. Based on our perceptions we form our own ideas on how things "should" be. We believe that things need to be a certain way and place requirements on others, ourselves, and situations to be the way we want it to be or we *pitch a fit or blame others for our situation.*

We place the responsibility of our happiness in outside influences for which we have little to no control; like the weather being nice for my camping trip, or the mood of my boss, or my kids minding me. It's no wonder there are so many unhappy people in the world. This belief can cause us serious grief and turmoil as we interact with others.

How often do we find ourselves in a disagreement over opinion? Sometimes we have the expectation that others need to see things exactly how we do.

Because we only see things from our own perception, and we like to be right, it can be very difficult to see another's view. This is one of the issues we struggle with throughout life because we constantly must deal with things with which we don't agree. We argue everything, trying to convince others that we are right. We waste so much time arguing and we wind up damaging relationships. The saying that captures this is old: "A person convinced against their will is of the same opinion still." Very seldom do we convince others that our way is "best."

We also have unrealistic expectations for ourselves. Sometimes we think we need to be perfect so that others will approve of us. Sometimes we expect others to be perfect so we will approve of them. If this happens, it is usually because we "project" our own expectations onto someone else. We see this play out in a parent/child relationship, where the parent is very hard on the child because of the way they performed for their sporting event or a piano recital. The parent is usually trying to relive their own childhood through their children, expecting them to succeed where they "failed." When we place our own hidden agenda on others it creates tension and stress; it ruins relationships.

What if we were able to let go of our requirements of others? How might that impact relationships? What if we were able to let go of our requirements for ourselves? Wouldn't that be AWESOME! But let's be realistic. If we didn't put any requirements on our children to get good grades or to do their best, then it could definitely get out of control. I think the key is finding a balance so we form expectations and set requirements which are stable and malleable, so when these are not met, we can approach the situation with a calm, healthy perspective; one that is more forgiving and less critical.

We are most judgmental of the people we love; expecting them to be perfect. Though we can be very critical of others, we are even more demanding of ourselves. We are much more lenient when others make a mistake. If we could reflect that leniency back onto ourselves, I believe our stress levels and overall mental health would be better.

If a child struggles in school to get good grades because a parent set the expectation of all A's, or B's, this may not be realistic for the child. A more balanced approach like expecting the child to complete and turn in all assignments regardless of the score, setting requirements a child can achieve. By setting reasonable expectations, we allow others the latitude to achieve success.

EMOTIONS

As long as we have access to our logic, we make pretty responsible decisions. If we make decisions while we are emotional, situations often turn out negatively.

There is a wonderful presentation on emotions specifically anger, entitled "Anger as a Fear Driven Emotion" by Lauren Murphy Payne, MSW. Her premise states that we only have two emotions: love and fear, and all other emotions derive from these. This idea breaks things down to a simple formula used to understand how we communicate with others and how others communicate with us. Generally, we can feel the difference between loving communication and fearful communication. Anger is one defense mechanism for our fears. But it's not only anger; it's any coping strategy we want to use - substance abuse, gambling, addiction, shopping, cutting, eating disorders, etc.   When we feel insecure or vulnerable, we get defensive about it. These defense mechanisms originate from five basic fears every person has experienced, as follows:

The fear of getting hurt physically or emotionally.
Example: I get angry when my partner walks out on me after a fight. **Mental Pause**: take a deep breath, or go for a walk. Realization: The anger I'm feeling is based on my fear of getting hurt emotionally.

The fear of being inadequate.
Example: After telling your child to clean their room a few times you start to get angry because he or she is not doing what you asked. **Mental Pause**: Take a deep breath and ask , why am I really angry? What am I scared of? Realization: I'm actually scared and fearful of not being adequate or good enough as a parent.

The fear of being abandoned.

Example: Your partner tells you he or she will be home at 7:00. It is now 8:30 and they are not home and they haven't called. You begin to feel angry, but what is your real feeling? **Mental Pause**: Take a deep breath. The anger could be rooted in worry, frustration, disrespect, or jealousy. Realization: These feelings could stem from a fear of abandonment.

The fear of losing ourselves. Not being able to do the things we want, having to give up our own interests, forfeiting ourselves for another. Example: My father has cut my hair ever since I was a child. When my son was eight and my dad was cutting my hair, I tried to get my son to let grandpa cut his hair. My son declined and the more I tried to get him to do it, the more upset he got. Years later I asked him why he didn't let grandpa cut his hair? He said he was worried about his friends teasing him because his haircut would look like mine. I guess a kid with a full head of hair wouldn't want to trade it for a half a head of hair and a receding hairline. **Mental Pause**: Why was my son getting upset? Realization: He had the fear of losing himself and not being the person he wanted to be.

The fear of hurting others physically or emotionally.

Example: You walk out of the grocery store with your three-year-old who refuses to hold your hand. S/He starts running out into the road so you grab her/him and proceed to yell at the child. **Mental Pause**: Breathe deeply. Why am I angry? Realization: I have the fear of my child getting hurt which is fueling my anger.

If we analyzed our communication and our behavior over the last year or so, we would more than likely come to the conclusion that we operate out of fear most of the time. Every time we make an emotional decision, it has a root in one or more of these fears. If we are operating out of love, then we are feeling peace, respect, and confidence. If we are operating out of fear, then we are feeling aggressive, frustrated, jealous, and anxious. Paying attention, it becomes very easy to recognize how we communicate and how others communicate with us. When we become aware, we can choose what to do with it.

We can gain control of ourselves, rather than responding emotionally. Learning how to raise tolerance and confidence levels to those five fears helps us deal with anger or other maladaptive coping strategies in a more effective manner.

Sometimes it is helpful when we begin to feel anger and ask ourselves "Why am I really angry? What am I scared of right now?" The more we do this the better we get at pinpointing the source of the anger.

For more information about "Anger as a Fear Driven Emotion" please email Lauren Murphy Payne at lmpandassoc@gmail.com.

CONFIDENCE

The topic of confidence is a common theme in the decision making process. Confidence is when we are assured that as an individual we can succeed; a lack of confidence creates a poor self image leading to even less confidence. Many people struggle to some degree with a lack of confidence directly linked with the fear of inadequacy. If we lack confidence in our self-worth, it impacts the way we interact with others and make decisions.

But what if this lack of confidence is another misperception? An illusion in our mind? For example; We have a newborn child and we bring him/her home. Immediately, we start sending messages to him/her about her/his value. These messages are seeds which form the newborn's values and beliefs.

These messages hit the infant with the same power and effect of a baseball bat swung at a mattress. Messages received may be positive or negative.

Being told as children that we couldn't do something because we were too little, that we were bad because we spilled milk, that we would never amount to anything, we were worthless, all are messages we absorb, and from these messages, we form our identity and self worth.

The mattress is pretty resilient for a while and holds its form despite being hit with the bat. But after experiencing these situations for twenty, thirty, forty years, there is a pretty big divot in that mattress. This divot is a lack of confidence, or the fear of inadequacy.

But what if this fear "divot" is only an illusion, a belief we adopted from others? The reality is we are ALL good enough and we ALL deserve to have good things in our lives. For those who have children in your lives, think about when they were infants. What was their worth based on?

It certainly couldn't be based on the amount of money they made, or the car they drove, or the clothes they wore. They have intrinsic value, simply because they are their authentic selves. There is nothing they need to "do" to earn our love. But as the baby grows and learns and experiences they begin to doubt their worth, and instead, place their worth in accumulating material things or more damaging behaviors.

Teenagers demonstrate this concept perfectly, always needing to have the latest fashions and being part of the coolest trends. Adults do this as well. We are very good at using various coping strategies (substance use, shopping, gambling, eating disorders, cutting) so that we don't have to deal with the fear of inadequacy.

But remember, fear is an *illusion*. The infant's worth never changed based on what they did or didn't do, so how can our worth change? It can't! Because the reality is that we are all a bunch of grown up babies! Regardless, we cannot say or do anything to alter our intrinsic worth as human beings. Learning to love ourselves the way we love our babies is crucial to living happily. If we do not have babies in our lives, a comparison could also be made to a close friend or even a pet.

We spend a lifetime learning to accept the world as others see it. We are information sponges from the time we are born (actually, in utero). Our processes and experiences form our core values and beliefs. Sometimes understanding our values and beliefs can be difficult as we don't pay consistent attention to the more intangible, internalized matters. An easy way to figure out what our beliefs are is to look at our lives.

Our outside world is a reflection of who we are inside. Who are we inside? Our values and beliefs, perceptions, feelings and thoughts. So if we are confused about what we believe, all we have to do is look at our life. Everything in our life is a manifestation of what we believe.

A belief is a repetitive thought regarding inner values. To change any aspect of our lives, we first need to examine the belief responsible for creating a specific behavior. Then we may work on changing that belief such that our reality will change in that situation.

LIVING THE SERENITY PRAYER

*"God grant me the serenity to accept
the things I cannot change; the courage to change
the things I can and the wisdom to know the
difference."*

There is a lot of wisdom in this short phrase which basically mentions two points: 1. Things that I cannot change or things outside of my control, and 2. Things I can change or things within my control.

What is it that I can control? My actions and reactions to situations. That is it! Everything else, according to the Serenity Prayer, must simply be accepted. Acceptance doesn't mean "agree," acceptance means "I accept the fact I have no control over this." We have all tried to "control things outside of our control" before. Ever tried to keep a small child quiet in the store? Or get them to clean up their mess?

These situations are very frustrating because we don't get to necessarily attain our desired outcome, which frustrates us even more. It has a snowball effect, and ultimately emotions get blown out of proportion and we do or say unsavory things we later regret.

If we were able to apply the wisdom of the "Serenity Prayer," then we would have a balance and be able to recognize the situations we have no control over, accept it and let go. I have observed individuals getting physically aggressive because of how strongly they feel about a particular subject. The problem is that they have little control over the outcome. A good example of this is the presidential election. The amount of influence we have here basically consists of voting for the candidate we think is the best. Outside of that, we have no control; so if we are applying the "Serenity Prayer," then we just accept the rest and let it go. How many times have we watched a riot break out at a sporting event over who really won? How much control do individuals have here? Zilch!

Then we look back and see how ridiculous it was to act that way. Finding the balance of changing what we can and letting go of the rest, is vital. That's easy to say, right? This is a major societal problem that leads to chaos and crisis, from verbal disagreements to child abuse to domestic violence to religious and political disputes to wars and so on.

The more someone tries to control something outside their realm of control, the more frustrated and angry they become. They become more and more drastic in their attempts to manipulate others into getting what they want. And succeeding.

To live the "Serenity Prayer" eliminates stress from our lives. According to https://www.stress.org/stress-and-heart-disease/, the number one killer in the United States is heart disease, and the number one contributor to heart disease is stress. If we look at our life situations through the wise lens of the "Serenity Prayer;" a situation may be under my control so I take care of it (no stress), or it can be out of my control so I accept the situation for what it is (no stress). That is pretty powerful. By applying this principle and increasing the range of our perspective, we significantly reduce our risk of getting heart disease, as well as many other ailments related to stress.

TAKING MISTAKE AND FAILURE OUT OF YOUR VOCABULARY

A common feeling for every person is that we feel bad when we make a mistake. Depending on how big a mistake we make, we can hold on to that guilt or grief for an hour or ten years or even indefinitely. People talk about how they "failed a test" or left a relationship because it was abusive. They feel guilty and ashamed for being with that person in the first place; believing they were "so stupid to make that kind of mistake." It doesn't really matter what we do, we can always find something to criticize.

If we eliminate the words "Mistake and Failure" from our vocabulary and replaced them with "Learning Opportunity" much would change. I didn't fail the test, I had an opportunity to learn something new. I was in that abusive relationship to learn what I want and don't want in a relationship and how to set appropriate boundaries. People say, "I set myself up for failure." How about, "I set myself up for a learning experience."

Think back to when you were in grade school. We didn't start kindergarten knowing all the answers. When we were learning to spell "cat," we probably spelled it "kat" a few times before we got it correct. This is the natural humanistic learning process. Just because we made a "mistake" on our spelling test doesn't mean anything other than it allows us another chance to strengthen our weaknesses. We generally don't feel guilty or shameful when these types of things happen in school, but if a child does experience these feelings it is likely because of unrealistic expectations placed on them from someone else. As we get older we put additional demands on ourselves with academics, work, and family responsibilities. We even put demands on our appearance and when we don't meet those expectations, we can be pretty hard on ourselves.

If we perceive life as our "Life School," then these "mistakes" we make just become an opportunity to improve. Some lessons are more difficult to learn than others. Until it is resolved, a situation keeps repeating itself over and over again. Once we learn the lesson, that specific situation stops, and we move on from it to our next lesson. We are all products of our experience; we wouldn't be who we are today had we not gone through these experiences.

If there is no such thing as failures and mistakes, then there is no reason to feel guilty or ashamed. We can just receive the lesson. There's no need to be critical as we haven't made any mistakes. Wouldn't it be great to let go of self judgment? When we free ourselves of self-judgment, guilt and shame, we eliminate negative emotions that substantially influence our decision-making. Imagine a world without guilt, shame, and stress. Hard to imagine? I think it would be pretty amazing to live in that world; and we can do that by shifting our perspective from criticism to serenity.

ATTITUDE IS EVERYTHING

When I was going to Weber State University for my bachelors' degree, I remember taking a class in a stadium style classroom. What I remember most was a banner that hung from the ceiling. It was bright red with white capital letters:

ATTITUDE IS EVERYTHING

This statement intrigued me. As I completed my studies, I went into the sales field learning that whether or not I sold anything largely depended on my attitude. If I went to a customer with the mindset that I already sold them the product and I had the solution to their problem, the chances of me closing the deal was much higher than if I went in with doubt or criticism or lack of confidence. I would think of this phrase often as I interacted with others and was also amazed how influential I became because of my attitude. As I left the sales field, and started working as a corrections officer at a prison, I carried this thought with me and I experienced that the inmates generally responded to me based on the attitude I had. If I was pleasant and respectful, so were they for the most part. If I was confrontive or combative, I was met with resistance, hostility and anger. I noticed the impact this new attitude had on my family and friends, on all my interactions. I could actually control, or at least influence, what happens to me and my family based on my attitude. Twenty years later after sitting in that class looking up at that sign, I can truly say that for me attitude is EVERYTHING!!

LIVING LIFE ON PURPOSE

"There are people who make things happen, there are people who watch things happen, and there are people who wonder what happened. To be successful, you need to be a person who makes things happen."

Jim Lovell

Some people are successful and seem to have everything they want, while others struggle to pay the rent and put food on the table. So what makes the difference between the rich and the poor? The situation we are born into certainly sets the stage and has a profound effect on our beliefs and perceptions, but once we become adults we are able to view things however we want and do whatever we want. Just because we were born into a certain situation doesn't mean we have to stay there. We can do everything or we can do nothing; as adults the choices become ours to make.

My son came home from school shopping with a t-shirt that read "I'm not lazy, I just really enjoy doing nothing." We are all motivated to do something, even if it is nothing. What gets you really excited? What are you most passionate about? Everyone is born with talents. What are your talents and how can you adapt more of those activities into your life? If I was an artist and liked to paint, I might try to make my living through my art. There are people who achieve this goal but the reality is that there are a lot of starving artists. We still have to live life, earn money, pay bills, the usual stuff.

So how can we live our lives on purpose? By finding ways to incorporate our passions into our lives. Just because we can't make a living with our dreams doesn't mean they aren't important. Finding ways to fill life with passion and purpose helps us all to feel good about what we are doing and accomplishing.

Here are some tools to help regulate emotions, gain confidence, clear emotional blocks, and make internal changes:

Reading/Self Help Books

Meditation

EFT/Tapping

Reiki

Holotropic Breathwork

Sauna/ Sweat Lodge

Exercise

Journaling

Creative Expression

Art Work

Crafts

MENTAL PAUSE

PART III

The Mental Pause Formula

MENTAL PAUSE

PUTTING IT ALL TOGETHER

Now that I have given you all this
information, how can we put it to use? Here is the
prescription:

1. Notice when the body shows signs of
    emotionality (increased heart rate, sweats,
    headaches, tunnel vision etc)

2. Upon noticing the body's warning signs, we
    must tell ourselves **"I need to go through a
    Mental Pause."**

3. Find some open space or window. Take
    some deep breaths, calm down, **DO NOT
    REACT!**

4. Once the body begins to calm, we search
    internally, rationally, at our options.
    (Remember, if you only see one option, it is
    the wrong one!)

5.   Choose the best option that both solves the problem and doesn't cause negative consequences for ourselves or those around us.

Sometimes it is helpful to utilize a "Thinking Report" to analyze a negative situation. This tool is useful for analyzing situations that have already occurred, those moments that we look back and think of what we could have done differently. There are many variations of a Thinking Report as it is readily available via internet, and once we become familiar with them, we can create ones which focus on specific needs. It is comprised of a few basic elements. First, the situation is written down on paper. What was my behavior? Then list all of the thoughts and feelings experienced at the time the incident occurred. Then list the underlying belief which justified the thoughts.

Once these things are written down, go back and identify what risk thoughts and feelings most likely justified the behavior. Then brainstorm new ways of thinking that would keep you from engaging in negative behavior. Then apply the new thinking. How would that have changed the situation?

Example:

Taking the ACT to get accepted into college.

Situation:

I cheated on a test

Thoughts:

I need to score high on this test

I should have studied harder

What will people think of me if I get a low score?

Maybe no one will notice me cheating

I could get away with it

I know this stuff, I'm just really bad at taking tests

Feelings:

Frustrated, anxious, scared, worried, embarrassed

Core Value:

I need to be accepted

I need to perform well

I need to be perfect

Remember the iceberg diagram? If we go back over the Thinking Report it would be possible to identify risk thoughts and feelings. The thoughts that most likely led to the cheating was "what will people think of me?" and "I could get away with it." The risk feelings might be scared or embarrassed and my risk belief would be "I need to be perfect." The belief leads to feelings, feelings lead to thoughts, thoughts lead to actions, and actions lead to consequences.

The next step is to brainstorm new ways of thinking like "why does it matter what people think of me?" Sometimes it's easier to add onto an existing thought rather than try to replace it. I could just add onto the end of the risk thought. "I could get away with it" with "but it's not worth it." This phrase helps take energy that particular thought held and defuse it.

Utilizing a **"mental pause"** to break up the decision making process has been an amazing tool for me as it has helped me maintain control of my life. It has allowed me to live the life I want to live. My hope is that it can do the same for you.

.

ABOUT THE AUTHOR

Brandon lives in Roy Utah with his beautiful wife and has five wonderful children. He works for the Utah Department of Corrections as a mental health therapist. He also has a private counseling practice. He earned his Bachelor's Degree in Technical Sales and Marketing in 1999 from Weber State University. He then went on to get his Master's Degree in Clinical Mental Health Counseling from the University of Phoenix in 2012. He loves to spend time with his family and enjoys being in nature. He is passionate about helping others discover who they are so they can live their lives authentically.